SNAPSHOTS IN HISTORY

THE BERLIN WALL

Barrier to Freedom

by Michael Burgan

THE BERLIN WALL

Barrier to Freedom

by Michael Burgan

Content Adviser: Tom Lansford, Ph.D., Assistant Dean and
Associate Professor of Political Science, College of Arts and Letters,
University of Southern Mississippi

Reading Adviser: Katie Van Sluys, Ph.D.,
School of Education, DePaul University

Compass Point Books ✦ Minneapolis, Minnesota

✦ COMPASS POINT BOOKS

3109 West 50th Street, #115
Minneapolis, MN 55410

Visit Compass Point Books on the Internet at
www.compasspointbooks.com
or e-mail your request to
custserv@compasspointbooks.com

For Compass Point Books
Jennifer VanVoorst, Jaime Martens, Lori Bye, XNR Productions, Inc.,
Catherine Neitge, Keith Griffin, and Nick Healy

Produced by White-Thomson Publishing Ltd.

For White-Thomson Publishing
Stephen White-Thomson, Susan Crean, Amy Sparks,
Tinstar Design Ltd., Tom Lansford, Peggy Bresnick Kendler,
Brian Fitzgerald, Barbara Bakowski, and Timothy Griffin

Library of Congress Cataloging-in-Publication Data
Burgan, Michael.
  The Berlin Wall : barrier to freedom / by Michael Burgan.
    p. cm. — (Snapshots in history)
  ISBN-13: 978-0-7565-3330-4 (library binding)
  ISBN-10: 0-7565-3330-9 (library binding)
1. Berlin Wall, Berlin, Germany, 1961-1989—Juvenile literature.
2. Berlin (Germany)—History—1945-1990—Juvenile literature.
3. Germany—History—1945-1990—Juvenile literature. 4. Cold
War—Juvenile literature. I. Title. II. Series.
  DD881.B735 2008
  943'.1552087—dc22   2007004909

$23.99 NOV 2007

 This book was manufactured with paper containing
at least 10 percent post-consumer waste.

CONTENTS

A City Divided

Just after midnight on Sunday, August 13, 1961, Adam Kellett-Long sat at his office typewriter. The young British journalist worked in East Berlin, the capital of the German Democratic Republic, also called East Germany. At the time, Germany was divided into two nations—East Germany and the Federal Republic of Germany, or West Germany. The city of Berlin was split as well. As Kellett-Long worked, his phone rang. A voice he did not know spoke to him in German. In English, the words meant, "A small suggestion—don't go to bed tonight!" After speaking that one line, the caller hung up.

For several days, Kellett-Long had been thinking that something important was going to happen in Berlin. Now the mysterious phone call led him out of his office and into his car. He drove toward the border between East Berlin and West Berlin. A member of the Volkspolizei, or People's Police, waved him away. Continuing along the deserted streets, Kellett-Long found a soldier holding a red light. He, too, would not let the reporter past. The soldier told him that the border was closed.

Armed East German guards prevented people from crossing the border between East Berlin and West Berlin.

At that moment, armed soldiers and police officers were hard at work across East Berlin. Trucks carrying concrete posts and rolls of barbed wire moved up to the border that separated East Berlin and West Berlin. The soldiers and police pounded the posts into the ground and strung the wire between them. The political division of Berlin into two halves, east and west, was now an actual physical division. The barbed-wire fence, and the armed guards who stood by it, shut off the flow of traffic and people between East Berlin and West Berlin.

Kellett-Long was one of the first people to know that life was about to drastically change in Berlin. Others soon learned. The underground and surface trains that ran between the two halves of the city were stopped. At the last station on the eastern side, West German riders were told to get off the trains and find their own way home. Along the border, armed troops moved into position. They refused to let East Berliners into the western half of the city.

As the morning came, the whole city realized what had happened during the night. People gathered on both sides of the barbed-wire fence. Margit Hosseini was a young West Berliner who went to the fence that day. At the time, her sister was staying with relatives just outside East Berlin. She later remembered:

It was terrible, people crying, shouting, some were frightened, some were angry, and I just remember I was so frightened. I thought we would never see my sister. She's lost, so to speak.

Friends and family suddenly found their lives separated by a barbed-wire fence.

An Eyewitness Report

U.S. journalist Daniel Schorr was working for the Columbia Broadcasting System (CBS) when the Berlin Wall first went up. On the morning of August 13, 1961, he told his CBS Radio listeners: "I toured East Berlin today and found it an armed camp. Police and troops with machine guns everywhere hold back the ... population ... Russian and East German tanks in reserve. ... My cameraman and I were arrested and held for 90 minutes, our film confiscated [taken away]. ... I saw hundreds of confused and resentful East Germans being turned away from subway and train stations, some arrested for shouting."

The people of Berlin would no longer be able to move freely, and East Berliners faced arrest—or worse—if they tried to enter West Berlin. Within days, the barbed-wire fence was replaced with a solid concrete wall, soon to be known as the Berlin Wall. Berliners knew then that their city would remain divided in half.

Since World War II ended in 1945, Berlin had been a center of conflict. On one side were the United States and its allies, with the Soviet Union on the other. During the war, the Americans, British, French, and Soviets had united to defeat Germany. After the war, they divided Germany into four zones and the city of Berlin into four sectors. By 1948, all zones except the one controlled by the Soviet Union had been united to create West Germany. The Soviet zone became East Germany.

Berlin sat deep within East Germany. Even with the creation of two separate German states,

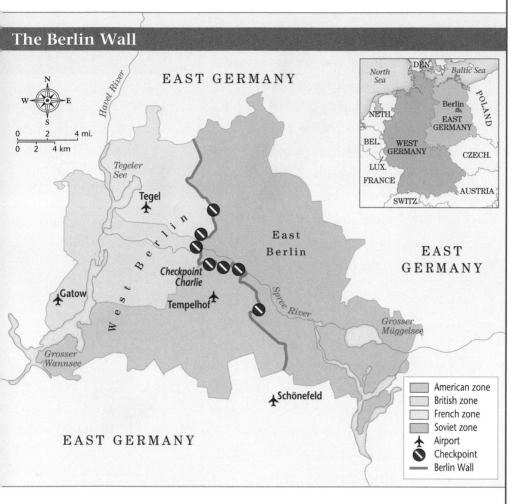

The Berlin Wall

EAST GERMANY

EAST GERMANY

EAST GERMANY

East Berlin

West Berlin

Havel River

Tegeler See

Tegel

Gatow

Checkpoint Charlie

Tempelhof

Spree River

Grosser Müggelsee

Grosser Wannsee

Schönefeld

N
W E
S

0 2 4 mi.
0 2 4 km

North Sea · DEN. · Baltic Sea
NETH. · Berlin · POLAND
BEL. · WEST GERMANY · EAST GERMANY
LUX. · FRANCE · CZECH.
SWITZ. · AUSTRIA

American zone
British zone
French zone
Soviet zone
✈ Airport
◐ Checkpoint
— Berlin Wall

the United States and other allies kept the legal right to control their sectors in Berlin. They set up a democratic government, as they had in West Germany. The Soviets, meanwhile, created a Communist state in East Germany, with East Berlin as its capital. Under communism, only one political party, the Communist Party, controlled the government. The economy was based on socialism, with the government owning most businesses and property. People had almost no freedom to do what they pleased.

Berlin was a divided city within a divided country.

13

At that time, the Soviet Union wanted to spread communism around the world. The United States and its allies wanted to combat the spread of communism and promote democracy. The decades-long conflict between the two sides was called the Cold War.

Hundreds of thousands of East Germans disliked living in a Communist state, so they came to East Berlin and then crossed over into West Berlin. From there, they could travel to West Germany or other democratic countries. The Berlin Wall was eventually put up in order to stop this flow of people from East Germany to the West. Border guards kept watch for anyone trying to get over the wall.

On August 15, 1961, the permanent wall was not yet up. Just the original barbed-wire fence separated the two halves of the city. On that day, a young border guard named Conrad Schumann stood in East Berlin next to the barbed wire. He heard West Berliners shouting at him. They called him and the other guards pigs and traitors because they would

THE COLD WAR

In 1946, U.S. journalist Herbert Bayard Swope became the first person to use the term "cold war" to describe the growing tensions between the Soviet Union and the United States. Neither country wanted to use its troops directly against the other in what Swope called a "hot" war. But the two foes sent weapons and money to their allies, which sometimes battled each other. And in some cases, U.S. troops fought foreign soldiers supported by the Soviets, as in Vietnam. Swope called this indirect conflict a "cold" war. Soon other journalists began using the phrase as well.

not let East Berliners cross into the West. Then Schumann heard another shout: *Freheit*—"liberty." He knew that the East German government was trying to end some of the last freedoms the people enjoyed. He also knew a bigger and stronger wall would soon be built. With the West Germans reminding him of what he would soon lose, he decided to act. Schumann stepped onto and over the barbed wire. A photographer captured the moment when Schumann made his leap to freedom, and soon it was seen around the world.

East German soldier Conrad Schumann gained his freedom by leaping over the barbed-wire barrier that was erected on August 13, 1961.

East German workers joined soldiers and guards in building the first concrete sections of the Berlin Wall.

Once the concrete wall was put up, it did its job well. In the beginning, however, dozens of East Germans managed to sneak past the barrier and find their freedom. But in the years to come, several hundred people were shot as they tried to cross into West Berlin.

The wall between East Berlin and West Berlin was 26¾ miles (43 kilometers) long. Another barrier ringed West Berlin, cutting it off from the East German countryside that surrounded it. For almost 30 years, these walls kept East Germans from visiting the West. But in 1989, the Soviet Union began to loosen its control over East Germany and other Communist nations of Eastern Europe. With the Cold War reaching its end, the Berlin Wall finally came down, and Germany was soon united again. The small bits of the wall that still stand today remind the world of the long struggle for freedom so many Europeans endured. ◣

Breaking Up Berlin

Chapter

2

The loss of freedom was on the minds of many Europeans decades before the Berlin Wall went up. In the early morning hours of September 1, 1939, the huge guns of a German battleship began firing on the Polish city of Danzig, known today as Gdansk. Within hours, German tanks and troops crossed the border into Poland while German planes streaked across the sky. From his capital in Berlin, German leader Adolf Hitler had begun his conquest of Europe, and the German invasion of Poland marked the official start of World War II.

Thousands of miles away, U.S. President Franklin Roosevelt watched the outbreak of war with concern. He knew that most Americans wanted to stay out of another European war, after having lost more than 100,000 men during

German tanks easily overran Polish defenses in the opening days of World War II.

World War I. But Roosevelt also knew that Hitler presented a danger to U.S. allies in Europe, such as France and Great Britain. Hitler ruled as a dictator and had already taken control of Austria and Czechoslovakia. He also denied legal rights to German Jews and had already sent some of them to concentration camps.

Over the next 18 months, Hitler's forces marched across Western Europe, taking control of Denmark, Norway, Belgium, the Netherlands, and France. Then, in June 1941, Hitler turned east and invaded the Soviet Union. Roosevelt had already sent weapons and supplies to Great Britain. Now the United States began to aid the Soviet Union as well, even though most Americans disliked and distrusted its communist system. They knew

NAZISM AND THE HOLOCAUST

Adolf Hitler was the head of the National Socialist German Workers' Party. The party's members were known as Nazis. Hitler thought Germans were part of a master race that was superior to any other race or ethnic group. He particularly detested Jews, who he thought were the root of all of Germany's troubles. Hitler's government began sending some Jews to concentration camps. Once World War II started and Germany invaded other nations, the Nazis rounded up the Jews in each country and sent them to the camps. Some of the camps were turned into death camps, where tens of thousands of Jews were killed. By the war's end, about 6 million Jews were dead. Non-Jews were also sometimes killed at the death camps. This episode in history became known as the Holocaust.

that Soviet leader Joseph Stalin hoped to one day destroy capitalism, the economic system in the United States.

On December 7, 1941, Japan launched a surprise attack on the U.S. naval base at Pearl Harbor, Hawaii. Roosevelt asked Congress to declare war on Japan. Germany, which had diplomatic ties

On June 14, 1940, victorious German troops paraded past the Arc de Triomphe in Paris, the capital of France. All of France was soon under German control.

21

to Japan, then declared war on the United States. Now the Americans and Soviets were on the same side, fighting the Germans, aided by Great Britain and other nations.

On June 6, 1944, British, Canadian, and U.S. troops launched a land invasion against German forces in France. Within one year, the Soviets in

Starting on June 6, 1944, U.S. and Allied soldiers came ashore at several beaches in Normandy, France. They pushed east to defeat Nazi Germany.

the East and their Allies in the West closed in on Berlin. Hitler committed suicide in his bunker there on April 30, 1945. One week later, the war in Europe was over, and Japan surrendered in August 1945.

Earlier in 1945, Roosevelt, Stalin, and British Prime Minister Winston Churchill had discussed how to rule Germany once the Allies won. The country would be split into four zones, with Great Britain, France, the United States, and the Soviet Union each controlling one zone. Berlin would also be split four ways. Since Berlin was 110 miles (176 km) into the eastern, Soviet zone, Stalin agreed that the other Allies could travel through the zone to reach their sectors of the city.

The details of the four-way division of Germany were worked out in July 1945 in Potsdam, Germany. Roosevelt had died in April, and Harry Truman was now the U.S. president. Truman knew that Stalin resisted free elections and democratic governments in the parts of Eastern Europe his army controlled.

The Cold War emerged as Truman and his Western European Allies realized the Soviet Union would do anything to preserve its influence and spread communism. Winston Churchill said in 1946 that Stalin was putting up an "Iron Curtain" that separated the free, democratic nations of Europe from the growing communist influence in the East. The United States prepared to use its military and economic strength to protect democratic, capitalist countries and end communism wherever it existed.

The Iron Curtain

Winston Churchill served as prime minister of Great Britain two separate times for a total of 10 years. He was out of office in 1946, when he visited U.S. President Harry Truman's home state of Missouri. On March 5, at Westminster College in Missouri, Churchill gave one of the most famous speeches of the Cold War. He said, "From Stettin in the Baltic to Trieste in the Adriatic, an Iron Curtain has descended across the continent." Churchill was referring to the control the Soviet Union held over Eastern Europe, which cut it off from the freedom of the West. The image of an Iron Curtain lasted as a symbol of the divide between the East and the West. The idea of such a barrier finally became real in 1961, with the building of the Berlin Wall.

Clark Clifford, an aide to Truman, helped write a report about the Soviet aims and how the United States should respond. Clifford later recalled his main point:

> *We ended up the report by saying the policy of our country should be set, and clearly set. The Soviet Union constitutes a real menace to freedom in this world. Freedom in Europe, freedom in the United States. So we must prepare for it.*

Tensions between the United States and the Soviet Union soon reached a postwar peak in Germany. Since 1945, Stalin had hoped to reunite the four German zones and put a Communist government in control. France, Great Britain, and the United States wanted a reunited Germany, too, but with a democratic government. The three Western Allies knew Stalin would not accept this, so early in 1948 they began planning to merge their three zones into a separate country, called West Germany. Through spies, Stalin learned of this plan, and he set out to stop the Allies. Stalin focused his attention on Berlin.

The city had been badly damaged by Allied bombs and Soviet artillery during World War II. When the war ended, people struggled to find food and shelter, and disease was common.

During World War II, more than half the buildings in Berlin were destroyed or partially destroyed, and more than 1 million residents fled the city.

25

In the years after the war, Berliners slowly began to rebuild, and they relied on goods from outside the city to survive.

Stalin hoped that he could force the Allies to give up their plan to unite their zones and perhaps one day force the Allies to leave Germany altogether. Stalin's plan was to limit Allied access through the Soviet zone of Germany into Berlin. The Soviets began a blockade of West Berlin on June 24, 1948. No trains, trucks, or boats could enter the French, British, and American sectors.

General Lucius Clay was the military governor of the American zone. He called the blockade "one of the most ruthless efforts in modern times to use mass starvation for political coercion [force]."

Clay suggested using armed trucks to bust through the blockade, but Truman said no. He did not want to risk a war. Instead, Truman agreed to use an airlift to bring supplies into the western sectors of Berlin.

THE BERLIN AIRLIFT		
Country	Number of Flights	Total Tonnage of Cargo
U.S.	189,963	1,783,573 (1,605,216 metric ton
Great Britain	87,841	541,937 (487,743 metric tons)
France	424	896 (806 metric tons)

For the next year, British, American, and a few French planes flew around the clock into West Berlin's airports, carrying food, coal, medical supplies, and other important goods. At the peak of the airlift, the planes brought in an average of almost 9,000 tons (8,100 metric tons) of supplies each day. At least 70 people died in plane crashes and other accidents connected to the airlift.

Some Allied pilots used tiny parachutes during the Berlin Airlift to drop candy to children waiting below.

27

Even with the aid, the citizens of Berlin struggled. They chopped down city trees for firewood, since the coal used to heat homes was in short supply. People didn't starve, but meals were often simple. Some families ate meat only twice a week. Many Berliners planted small vegetable gardens wherever they could and offered to trade household goods for food. West Berliners could still travel into the Soviet sector, and some went there to buy food. But most relied on the airlift, rather than deal with the Communists who controlled the other part of the city.

By May 1949, Stalin saw that his blockade had failed. The Allies were not leaving Berlin, and they were determined to keep the airlift going as long as possible. The Soviets agreed to lift the blockade; they received nothing from the Allies in return. By then, several changes had come to Europe. While the airlift was still going on, the Americans and their Allies had created the North Atlantic Treaty Organization (NATO). This military organization was designed to respond with force to any Soviet invasion of member countries.

In late May 1949, France, Great Britain, and the United States carried out their plan to create West Germany, which was officially known as the Federal Republic of Germany. The Soviets responded by making their zone the German Democratic Republic, or East Germany.

Also in 1949, the Soviet Union tested its first nuclear weapon. The United States had built and used the first of these weapons against Japan near the end of World War II. A single nuclear bomb could destroy large parts of a city and kill tens of thousands of people. With the Soviets developing these weapons, the United States faced an even more dangerous Cold War enemy.

Jubilant residents of Berlin waved to an American airlift plane following the announcement that the 11-month blockade would soon be lifted.

29

Life Under Communism

As 1949 drew to a close, Berlin remained split in two. Allied troops in the city and in West Germany defended the West Berliners from any Soviet or East German attack. The number of U.S. troops in Europe rose after June 1950, when North Korea, a Communist nation and Soviet ally, invaded South Korea, a U.S. ally. Some U.S. leaders feared the Soviet Union might launch a similar attack in West Berlin or West Germany.

Despite the Cold War, Berliners in all four sectors could still travel freely throughout the city. Even U.S. soldiers could venture into the Soviet sector. James Bourk, a private in the U.S. Air Force, said, "As long as you didn't cause any trouble or do anything wrong, they [the Communists] didn't bother you."

In the years after World War II, soldiers from the victorious Allied powers—including U.S. military police—stood guard throughout Berlin.

Every day, East Berliners saw that their half of the city differed sharply from West Berlin. West Germany was one of 16 nations to receive aid from the Marshall Plan. Under this plan, the United States gave money and goods to any European nation that asked for help. West Germany used some of its money to help rebuild West Berlin. The United States also gave direct aid to the city.

By 1953, some of these funds had helped create 150,000 new jobs in West Berlin. The rebuilding and rising wealth in West Berlin helped fuel the growth of stores. Meanwhile, East Berlin still looked grim and poor. Stalin wanted East Germany to provide the Soviet Union with steel, coal, and other crucial resources for its economy. East German leaders spent their money meeting the Soviets' demands, not the needs of their own people.

This policy of working for the Soviets was strengthened under Walter Ulbricht, who became the leader of East Germany in 1950. Ulbricht, like

CONFLICT IN THE SKIES

Although the Berlin Airlift ended peacefully, the Soviet Union continued to harass Allied planes and people in Berlin. In 1952, two Soviet fighter planes shot at a French commercial airliner as it flew along the air corridor over East Germany into West Berlin. The Soviets claimed the plane had left the corridor. Although two passengers were wounded, the plane landed safely. In another attack, the Soviets shot down a British warplane on a training mission. These attacks led the Allies to make diplomatic protests, but there were no further conflicts as a result of the attacks.

Stalin, ruled as a dictator. Under Ulbricht, a secret police service called the Stasi spied on East Germans and forced citizens to obey the ruling Communist Party. Citizens of East Berlin could only watch with despair as they saw West Berlin rebuild while they suffered.

Unlike East Berliners, the people of West Berlin had many choices when they went shopping for food and other goods.

One East Berlin construction worker described life in his city during 1953:

> *The average person lived very badly. If you're talking about the things everybody needs, like heating, coal, electricity, these things were all rationed. Electricity for domestic use was simply not available. The morale of the population dropped to zero.*

In 1952, the East German government had shut down the border between East Germany and West Germany. East Germans could move into West Germany only by passing through East Berlin.

Walter Ulbricht ruled East Germany for 21 years.

People from all over East Germany came to the capital so they could enter the American, British, or French sectors of the city. From there, they could move on to West Germany. The number of immigrants to West Germany rose after March 1953, when Joseph Stalin died. Many East Germans thought they should flee in case changes in the Soviet Union made their lives even harder. About 300,000 people left East Germany that year.

Changes did come in June 1953, when Ulbricht put even greater pressure on the workers of East Germany. The government raised the price of food while expecting the workers to produce more goods for the same pay. On June 16, workers in East Berlin protested the new demands, and soon the protest spread to other East German cities.

Within several days, 400,000 workers across the country were refusing to work, and many were also demanding greater democracy in the country. For a time, the Soviets shut off all entry into their sector of East Berlin. A report from the Central Intelligence Agency (CIA) noted, "This is the most complete isolation of West Berlin from the Russian [Soviet] zone that has yet been enforced."

Soviet leaders ordered tanks stationed in East Germany to roll into East Berlin and the other protest sites. The East Germans hurled stones as Soviet troops fired at them, killing about 50 protesters. Another 10,000 protesters were arrested as the Soviets restored order, and several hundred people were executed as punishment for disobeying the government.

After the June 1953 protests, the Soviets and East Germans publicly blamed the West for the trouble in East Berlin. They accused the Allies of wanting to start a war and weaken the East German government. The Allies denied that charge. In a

The 1953 protests against East Germany's Communist government spread from Berlin to more than 200 other towns.

LOCAL RADIO

In 1946, the U.S. military command in West Berlin created Radio in the American Sector (RIAS). It broadcast music, but its major goal was to give all Berliners accurate news, as opposed to the propaganda broadcast by the radio station in the Soviet sector. In 1953, RIAS reported on the protests in East Berlin. Radio listeners heard a report as the Soviet Union sent in its troops to end the protest: "It was horrible—the several salvoes [rounds of shots] that were fired, one after the other, how the people fell to the ground. We immediately saw some victims covered with blood, lying on the ground and obviously in pain. Everybody was calling for police and ambulances. Some of the victims were lifted onto police trucks and then rushed away for medical treatment."

statement to the Soviet military commander in East Berlin, the Western commanders wrote:

> *You and the rest of the world are well aware of the true causes of the disorders which have recently occurred in East Berlin, and it is ... unnecessary to tell you that the three powers in West Berlin had no responsibility whatever for instigating [starting] them.*

With tensions again on the rise between the Americans and the Soviets, Berlin took on a special role in the Cold War. Western spies could go into East Berlin to try to get information about Soviet and East German activities—and of course, the Communists did the same in West Berlin. Even before the June 1953 revolt, the Americans and British had begun working on a bold new plan to

37

spy on the Soviets in East Berlin. The code name given to this plan was Operation Stopwatch/Gold.

The secret plan united the CIA with the British Secret Intelligence Service (SIS). These two spy agencies worked together to dig a tunnel under the border between West Berlin and East Berlin. From inside the tunnel, agents tapped into Soviet communications and recorded messages. The tunnel went into operation in 1955, and over the next year the British and Americans recorded 50,000 reels of tape with Soviet messages.

In April 1956, East German soldiers appeared to accidentally discover the tunnel. A Soviet film crew recorded the East Germans as they explored the tunnel. The Soviets, however, had known about the tunnel all along, because they had a spy named George Blake working on Operation

SPY ON THE INSIDE

In April 1953, George Blake returned home to England. Blake, who worked for the British Secret Intelligence Service (SIS), had spent time in a North Korean prisoner-of-war camp during the Korean War. In England, Blake pretended to be a loyal SIS agent, but he was actually working for the Soviet Union. Blake's code name in Russian, Diomid (meaning "diamond"), suggested the value of his work to the Soviets. As part of his job with the SIS, Blake was involved in an early planning meeting for Operation Stopwatch/Gold. He told the Soviets about the tunnel and identified several hundred spies working for the Allies in East Germany. British officials learned in 1961 that Blake was a double agent. He was arrested and sent to prison. In 1966, Blake escaped and fled to the Soviet Union.

SIE TRETEN JETZT IN DIE AMERIKANISCHEN SEKTOR HINEIN

Stopwatch/Gold. The Soviets had let the tunnel go into operation. They feared if they shut the tunnel down before it opened, their spy's identity would be revealed.

The spying in Berlin did not end with the closure of the tunnel. Agents from both sides still sought information from their enemy. But to most East Berliners, spying was far removed from their lives. They were still trying to survive in a country where the Stasi followed almost all their moves, and the government demanded they keep working harder to aid the Soviet Union.

In April 1956, two policemen guarded an escape tunnel that had recently been discovered. They held a sign that translated roughly as "You are now in the American sector."

Struggle for Control

When East Germany shut its border with West Germany in 1952, it also cleared an area 3 miles (4.8 km) wide along the 860-mile (1,376-km) border. In this area, the East Germans strung barbed-wire fences and buried land mines. In watchtowers, armed guards searched for East Germans still bold enough to try to enter West Germany.

Throughout the 1950s, however, East Germans could still get to West Germany through West Berlin. Starting in 1953, people seeking freedom headed to the Marienfelde Refugee Center, in the southern part of the American sector of Berlin. Refugees came with only a few belongings or nothing at all. West German officials provided meals and a place to sleep for the refugees before they traveled by plane to West German cities.

In an effort to keep out East German spies, West German officials questioned people entering the Marienfelde Refugee Center. The center had beds for 3,000 people.

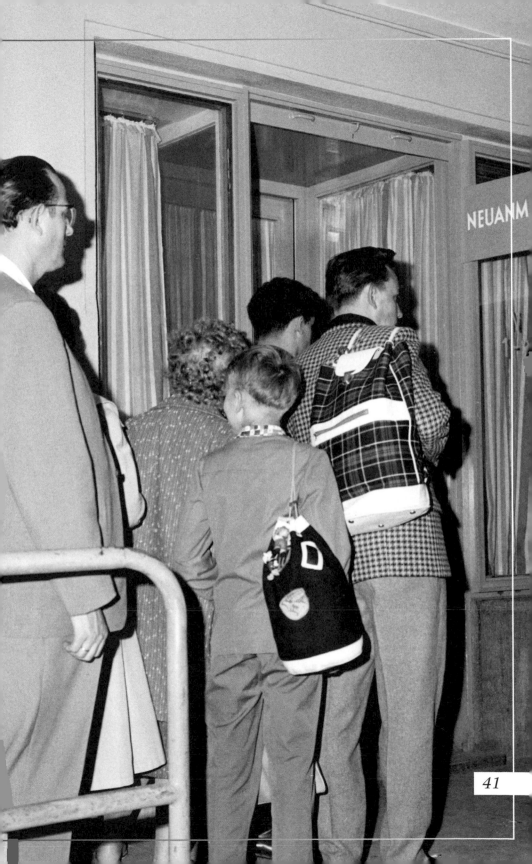

NEUANM

Between 1952 and 1959, the number of East German citizens heading west averaged more than 178,000 each year. They included tens of thousands of East Germany's best-educated workers: teachers, doctors, lawyers, and engineers. More than half of the people who fled were under the age of 25—the kind of young, skilled people Ulbricht needed to build his country's economy. In 1957, East Germany tried to crack down on the flight of refugees. The government made it a crime to head to West Germany, but the refugees had to be caught before they could be tried for that crime.

By this time, the Soviet Union had a new leader, Nikita Khrushchev. He, like Stalin, wanted a strong, Communist government in East Germany. The Soviet Union had suffered greatly during World War II, and Soviet leaders wanted to make sure Germany never attacked the country again. Having

NIKITA KHRUSHCHEV

A famous image of Soviet leader Nikita Khrushchev comes from the year 1960. While visiting the United Nations in New York, Khrushchev pounded the table with his shoe to show his anger with the West. At other times, Khrushchev boldly declared that communism would bury capitalism. Khrushchev was one of several Soviet leaders who struggled to gain power after Joseph Stalin's death, and he finally took control in about 1955. Despite his sometimes harsh words, Khrushchev did not want to fight the United States. He also tried to give his people slightly more freedom than they had had under Stalin, which was one reason why other hard-line Communist leaders forced him out of office in 1964.

an East German government that he could control, Khrushchev thought, would offer some protection from another invasion.

In November 1958, Khrushchev made a suggestion to deal with the situation in Berlin. The four nations that occupied Germany after World War II had never signed a peace treaty with Germany. Khrushchev thought it was time for the countries to sign treaties with the two Germanys. Then the four nations would have to pull their remaining forces out of Berlin. Khrushchev called the Allied presence in Berlin "a bone in our throat," and he was eager to remove it.

Although Nikita Khrushchev often spoke angrily about the United States and its allies, he also took steps to improve relations between his country and the West.

Two weeks later, Khrushchev went from offering a suggestion to making a demand. He told the Allies to leave Berlin within six months, or the Soviet Union would sign a separate peace treaty with East Germany and give it control of the Western sector. In the United States, Dwight D. Eisenhower was now president. He did not want the United States to leave West Berlin. But if a new peace treaty between the Soviet Union and East Germany was signed, all the earlier agreements Joseph Stalin

In 1959, Nikita Khrushchev (right) became the first Soviet leader to visit the United States. He toured New York, Hollywood, and several other spots before meeting with President Dwight D. Eisenhower.

had made about Berlin would no longer hold. The Allies would have to reach new agreements with the East Germans. They were not likely to continue to let the Allies travel through East Germany to West Berlin. The Allies did not want to recognize East Germany as a separate nation. They claimed that West Germany was the true government of the German people.

Khrushchev knew he had the Western Allies in a tight spot. "Every time I want to make the West scream," he said, "I squeeze on Berlin." But he, like Eisenhower, did not want to risk a war. In 1959, the two leaders met in Washington, D.C., and got along well. They agreed to meet again the next year to discuss the situation in Berlin. The improved relations, however, crumbled in May 1960, after the Soviet Union shot down a U.S. spy plane.

THE U-2 INCIDENT

In 1956, the United States began using a new plane to spy on the Soviet Union. The U-2 could reach altitudes of 75,000 feet (22,875 meters), out of the range of Soviet missiles. At that height, the plane's pilot used a high-powered camera to photograph Soviet military activity. On May 1, 1960, U.S. pilot Francis Gary Powers was flying a U-2 that was shot down over the Soviet Union. A new Soviet missile able to reach higher altitudes sent the plane crashing down to Earth. The Soviets captured Powers and sent him to jail. At first, U.S. President Dwight D. Eisenhower denied Powers was on a spy mission, but later he admitted it. In 1962, the Americans won Powers' release by swapping him for a captured Soviet spy.

As the arguing over Berlin continued, East Germans kept fleeing through West Berlin into West Germany. East Germans had food and basic housing, but they still had trouble getting other goods that were common in the West. A person in East Berlin who could afford to buy a refrigerator had to wait one year to actually get one. Cars were even harder to buy, since East German factories continued to make goods that went to the Soviet Union and other Communist nations. East German writer Stefan Heym later said:

> The people in the East looked toward the West with what I might say longing. They would have liked to have the same comforts, the same goods, the same chances, and they saw in ... socialism ... a system that demanded of them sacrifices, with nothing but promises for the future. And as long as the borders were open, it was relatively easy to get there.

Walter Ulbricht continued to push for a separate peace treaty with the Soviet Union. He was eager to take control of East Berlin and try to stop the flow of refugees. Khrushchev, however, wanted to go slowly. He thought he would have an easier time getting what he wanted with the new U.S. president, John F. Kennedy, who had been elected in November 1960.

Kennedy, however, wanted to be tough with the Soviets. They had just recently gained influence in Cuba, an island nation 90 miles (144 km) off the coast of Florida. Fidel Castro had taken power there in 1959 and was turning the country into a Communist state. After taking office, Kennedy approved an invasion of Cuba by anti-communist Cubans. With help from the CIA, these rebels launched the so-called Bay of Pigs invasion on April 17, 1961. The invasion was unsuccessful. After that failure, Kennedy was determined not to lose control in West Berlin.

Kennedy and Khrushchev met in Vienna, Austria, in June 1961. Berlin was their main topic. Once again, Khrushchev demanded that the four occupiers sign separate peace treaties with East Germany and West Germany. He also said the Allies must leave Berlin. Kennedy said the Allies would not give up their right to access Berlin. Khrushchev

More than 1,000 Cubans who took part in the failed Bay of Pigs invasion surrendered to Fidel Castro's soldiers.

John F. Kennedy and Nikita Khrushchev met in Vienna, Austria, to discuss the future of Berlin.

replied, "I want peace, but if you want war, that's your problem." Kennedy left Vienna determined to stand up to the Soviets. He asked Congress for $3 billion for the military. And he promised that the Americans would not leave Berlin.

On July 25, 1961, President Kennedy spoke to Americans about the growing crisis in Berlin. He said, in part:

> *It would be a mistake for others to look upon Berlin, because of its location, as a tempting target. The United States is there; the United Kingdom and France are there; the pledge of NATO is there—and the people of Berlin are there. ... We do not want to*

fight—but we have fought before. And others in earlier times have made the same dangerous mistake of assuming that the West was too selfish and too soft and too divided to resist invasions of freedom in other lands. ... We cannot and will not permit the Communists to drive us out of Berlin, either gradually or by force.

Even before the Vienna meeting, Ulbricht was calling on Khrushchev to take action. The flow of refugees had to stop. In March 1961, Ulbricht had proposed putting up barbed wire between East Berlin and West Berlin and putting more armed guards along the border. Khrushchev had told Ulbricht he could prepare to build a barrier.

At the end of July, one American suggested that could happen. Senator William Fulbright was the head of the Senate Foreign Relations Committee. He did not want Berlin to become the spot where the Cold War turned "hot," with fighting between the Allies and the Soviets. He said, "I don't understand why the East Germans don't close their border, because I think they have a right to close it."

President Kennedy had also said that he was concerned about the freedom and safety of West Berlin. He seemed to suggest that the Allies would not act if the Soviets did something on their own in East Berlin. On August 5, Khrushchev said that the East Germans could put up a barbed-wire fence. If the Americans did not respond with their military, then a permanent wall could go up. ◣

Building the Wall

In early August, while the Communist leaders met in Moscow, more than 1,000 East Germans headed across the border for the West each day. The number of refugees had increased after the Vienna conference, which was held in June 1961, when tensions between the United States and the Soviet Union seemed to be rising. To stop the flow, the East Germans put more troops along the border.

East Germany's government also tried to make life more difficult for East Berliners who worked in the western half of the city. Only people who worked in East Berlin were allowed to buy certain luxury items, such as cars or motorcycles. Still, on August 9, almost 2,000 people entered the Marienfelde Refugee Center.

In early August 1961, Germans living in both East Berlin and West Berlin were still permitted to drive their cars through the Brandenburg Gate, a Berlin landmark, to the other side of the city. That would change within a matter a days.

During the first week of August that year, some Allied intelligence agents began to wonder whether the Communists would try to seal off West Berlin. An East German doctor who also served as a local Communist official told the CIA that something could happen the weekend of August 13. Hartmut Wedel, an East Berlin dentist, had also heard local officials discussing the future of the city. He told agents, "They're going to erect barriers right in the middle of Berlin." Yet most Allied agents dismissed the idea of a wall going up through the city.

Across East Germany, some citizens knew their government was planning something big. Military and police units from the countryside were being sent to Berlin. But the details of the plan were kept secret, even within the East German government. Ulbricht put Erich Honecker in charge of building

A Spy's Problem

During the Cold War, one of the most important spies for the West was Soviet Colonel Oleg Penkovsky. He provided useful information about Soviet missiles that carried nuclear warheads. Penkovsky attended a dinner in Moscow on August 10, 1961—just four days before the Berlin Wall went up. He heard Nikita Khrushchev boast that the Soviets and East Germans were going to put up a barbed-wire fence "and the West will stand there like dumb sheep." Penkovsky knew he was hearing important news, but he wasn't sure he could safely pass along the information to the Central Intelligence Agency (CIA) without being caught. Besides, he doubted the West would be able to get the information in time to do anything to stop the Soviet plan. Penkovsky did not tell the CIA until September that he had learned about the wall in advance.

the barrier. Honecker was a dedicated Communist and the head of East Germany's national security forces. He and about 20 others were the only officials who knew exactly what was happening.

A few months before, Honecker had ordered troops to store barbed wire at a military base near Berlin. Concrete posts and barriers were placed at various sites within the city. When the time came, East German troops could quickly move the materials for the barrier into place.

Erich Honecker played a key role in building the Berlin Wall.

53

The order to act finally came in the early morning hours on Sunday, August 13. Soon, the elevated trains—the S-Bahns—and underground trains—U-Bahns—stopped running from East Berlin into West Berlin. Military trucks streamed into the city, carrying rolls of barbed wire and 40,000 troops. The soldiers and police officers would build the barrier and keep order. Soviet tanks also rumbled to the edges of the city, in case the Allies responded with an attack—or the citizens rose up in anger.

The East German officers and soldiers were not disturbed as they worked through the night. They cut down trees to use as barriers across some streets. In other places, they tore up the pavement so cars could not pass. The soldiers also set up concrete posts and strung barbed wire across them. A barbed-wire barrier also went around the 75-mile (120-km) border between West Berlin and the East German countryside. Through the night, small groups of West Berliners watched the barrier go up. They shouted insults, calling the soldiers swine, bums, and apes, among other names. The soldiers simply kept on working. On Saturday, there had been 80 checkpoints where people could pass from East Berlin to West Berlin and back. By Sunday morning, only 13 remained open, and armed guards limited who passed into and out of East Berlin.

During Saturday night, the East German government had issued a statement about the closing of the border. The Communists claimed

that the barrier was necessary to keep out spies and others who threatened the Communist government in the East. The Soviet government later said, "West Berlin authorities and the occupation organs of the three powers did not lift a finger to put an end to this criminal activity." The world knew, however, that the barrier was meant to keep in the East Germans who hungered for freedom.

Armed guards stopped people from passing through the border between East Berlin and West Berlin.

55

Wooden screens would keep Berliners from watching the building of the first concrete wall to cut through Berlin.

When the residents of Berlin woke up on Sunday morning, they saw that the barbed-wire fence was in place. Wooden barricades also blocked some streets. Families were now cut off from each

other, and East Berliners could no longer work or shop in the West. Even cemeteries were divided. Residents on one side of the barrier could not visit the graves of relatives on the other side.

Willy Brandt, the mayor of West Berlin, was out of town on the night of August 12. He returned on August 13 and angrily confronted some of the East German troops still tearing up the streets. The soldiers ignored him. Brandt also spoke to the Allied military commanders in West Berlin. They told him that they had orders not to take action. Brandt then understood the situation.

The United States and its allies would defend West Berlin if it were attacked, but they would not try to stop the building of the barrier. Some U.S. officials thought the barrier was actually a good thing. The flow of refugees from East Germany would halt, ending an issue that had caused problems between the Soviet Union and the United States. East German officials later called the wall the Friedensmauer—the Wall of Peace.

But Brandt and many Germans, in both East Berlin and West Berlin, did not welcome the Berlin Wall. In East Berlin, some residents tried to find ways through the barbed wire and checkpoints. On August 14, Daniel Schorr of CBS Radio reported that a handful of East Germans continued to break through to West Berlin. One man simply sped his car through a checkpoint; another kicked a guard in the stomach and then fled.

Margit Hosseini spent part of August 14 with her family, trying to find her sister who had been visiting relatives in East Berlin. During an S-Bahn trip, their train crossed through part of East Berlin. She remembered:

> *You had to drive through two stations still in East Berlin, where the train didn't stop ... on these stations there were all soldiers with machine guns. It was very frightening, really frightening. And only when we arrived in Papestrasse, which is now proper West Berlin, we were so relieved, really relieved—it was like the feeling of having escaped some danger.*

That same day, several thousand workers in West Berlin rallied to protest the lack of a response— diplomatic or military—from the Allies. About 250,000 people filled the streets on August 16. Some carried signs that accused the West of betrayal. Mayor Brandt spoke to the crowd. He told the people that he had written to President Kennedy. Egon Bahr, one of Brandt's aides, later said:

> *The idea was, since there had been no reaction in Washington, we had to make it clear to the president that there might be a breakdown in morale, a loss of trust. Something more than just a protest had to be done.*

On August 15, a crane had lowered a large slab of concrete along the border between East and West Berlin. Ulbricht and Honecker saw that the

Allies were not going to respond, and they went ahead with their plan to build a permanent wall. For the next week, more concrete was put into place. This concrete wall was 4 feet (1.2 meters) high, with barbed wire on top. It ran past the most famous landmark in Berlin, the Brandenburg Gate. At the gate and at other spots along the Berlin Wall, armed guards watched for any signs of escape.

On August 16, West Berlin Mayor Willy Brandt spoke for an hour to huge crowds that wanted the United States to take action against the Communists.

59

The Brandenburg Gate

The Brandenburg Gate has stood in Berlin for more than 200 years. At one time, it was one of a number of gates leading into the city, which was once the capital of a German state called Prussia. The gate's design was based on the entrance to the Acropolis, one of the most famous buildings of ancient Greece. On top of the gate is a statue called the Quadriga. The statue shows the goddess of victory riding in a chariot pulled by four horses. In 1806, the French dictator Napoléon Bonaparte defeated Prussia and took the Quadriga back to France. In 1814, the Prussians and their allies turned back Napoléon, and the Quadriga was returned to the gate. After that, the statue was firmly established as a symbol of German strength. With the division of Berlin after World War II, the Brandenburg Gate fell into the Soviet zone.

In the days before the concrete wall was finished, more East Berliners tried to get into West Berlin. In buildings that sat near the barbed wire, people jumped out of windows and over the barrier. West Berlin firefighters held blankets underneath them to break their fall. The East Germans responded by placing bricks in the windows that faced into West Berlin. One young couple stood kissing by the barbed wire. The man held wire cutters behind his girlfriend's back, snipping at the wires as they kissed. Once he had made an opening, the couple and dozens of other people dashed to freedom.

To show that he had not forgotten the people there, President Kennedy sent General Lucius Clay and Vice President Lyndon Johnson to West Berlin.

Clay, the hero of the Berlin Airlift, was now retired and served as Kennedy's personal representative in Berlin. The president also sent 1,500 more troops to West Berlin. Meanwhile, the building of the wall continued.

West Berliners tried to look over the Berlin Wall into East Berlin.

61

Face to Face at the Wall

Chapter

6

Within a few days of General Clay's arrival in Berlin, the East Germans tightened their grip on East Berlin. They reduced the number of checkpoints along the Berlin Wall from 13 to seven, and trains could cross at just one point. For a short time, West Berliners could still cross into East Berlin. Then, after August 23, the East Germans demanded that those entering East Berlin have special permits. The French, Americans, and British could enter East Berlin through just one spot, in the U.S. sector. This checkpoint was commonly called Charlie, the military term for the letter C.

In the first few weeks after the wall went up, East Germans continued to try to slip past the guards and cross the barriers. Some decided to escape without any planning. Seventeen-year-old

Soon after the Berlin Wall went up, Soviet and U.S. armed forces positioned tanks at the border crossing known as Checkpoint Charlie.

Ursula Heinemann found a spot where the border was still just marked with barbed wire. She fell to her stomach and crawled under the fence. The wire pulled at her clothes, and she scratched her hands, but she kept moving. Finally, a voice called to her and welcomed her to West Berlin. Another East Berliner managed to escape by hiding underneath an S-Bahn train. For about 30 minutes, he clung to metal bars under the train until it rolled into a West Berlin station.

In the days before the final concrete wall went up, some East Berliners made quick dashes to freedom, bringing to the West only what they could carry.

Not everyone who tried to escape reached West Berlin. The East German guards had received strong orders: "Border violators should be destroyed, and all attempts to breach the defenses should be prevented."

A young man named Gunter Litwin was shot and killed by border guards near the Berlin Wall on August 24, 1961. He was the first person killed trying to reach West Berlin. Others were caught before or during their escape attempts and sent to prison.

Through the end of summer and into the fall, people around the world feared the building of the Berlin Wall could spark a war. General Clay, although now retired, still saw himself as a general preparing for battle. Without any orders from U.S. officials, he tried to prepare U.S. troops for an assault on the wall. A U.S. military commander in West Berlin overruled Clay's decision.

On October 22, 1961, the threat of war seemed to rise. At Checkpoint Charlie, East German border guards stopped a U.S. diplomat. Under the past agreements between the Allies and the Soviet Union, the guards had no right to stop him or other U.S. officials. Clay and a U.S. general sent several tanks and other large military vehicles to the checkpoint. Under their protection, the diplomat entered East Berlin and then returned to West Berlin. The next day, Soviet and East German guards tried to stop another U.S. diplomat from

As tensions grew in October 1961, U.S. tanks moved into position along the wall near Checkpoint Charlie.

entering the Soviet zone. This time Clay sent 10 tanks. They stood at Checkpoint Charlie for several days, watching the flow of traffic into East Berlin.

On October 28, the Soviet Union reacted. It sent 30 tanks into East Berlin, and 10 moved opposite the U.S. tanks at Checkpoint Charlie. Colonel Jim Atwood was stationed in Berlin at the time. He later said:

The tensions escalated very rapidly for one reason, that this was Americans confronting Russians. It wasn't East Germans. There was live ammunition in both the tanks of the Russians and Americans.

By this time, President Kennedy was in secret contact with Khrushchev. The two leaders wanted to avoid conflict in Berlin. They soon agreed that first the Soviets would pull back their tanks, and the Americans would follow. Just before this, Khrushchev had dropped his demands that the Allies leave Berlin. A spy had told him that Kennedy was not ready to back down over Berlin. Still, the Soviets and East Germans were determined to cut off East Berlin from the West.

In August 1962, a new wall was erected behind the original concrete barrier. Between the two walls was an empty area, 100 yards (91 m) wide, called the Death Strip or No-Man's Land. Over time, the East Germans placed steel tank traps in the strip so vehicles couldn't cross it. Between the traps and the wall was a concrete road that East German vehicles used to patrol the wall. The Death Strip also had barbed wire and strips of gravel and sand. The strips were carefully raked so guards could easily spot the footprints of people trying to escape. And all along the wall the East Germans built guard towers and tiny concrete buildings called pillboxes. Inside them, armed guards prepared to shoot anyone who attempted escape.

West Berliners strolled along the Berlin Wall while, on the other side, guards and barriers kept East Berliners far from the wall.

On August 17, 1962, 18-year-old Peter Fechter was killed by East German guards. Fechter and a friend had approached the East Berlin side of the wall, not far from the U.S. soldiers manning

Checkpoint Charlie. The two young East Berliners dashed toward the wall. His friend made it into West Berlin, but bullets from the East German guards pierced Fechter's back and stomach. He fell not far from the wall and screamed in agony. U.S. soldiers and West Berlin civilians did not dare approach him; they feared they would be shot, too. Fechter bled to death. Fechter's death was more horrible than others at the wall. It happened in broad daylight, and Fechter died very slowly. For many, his killing came to represent the brutal nature of the Communists.

As work on the second Berlin Wall continued, a new crisis erupted between the Soviet Union and the United States. On October 16, 1962, a U-2 spy plane photographed Soviet missiles being set up in Cuba. The missiles could carry nuclear warheads to almost every major city in the United States. President Kennedy was determined to force Khrushchev to remove the missiles. But Kennedy feared starting a major war. "If they don't do anything in Cuba," he said, "they'll certainly do something in Berlin."

In Berlin, families prepared for a possible conflict. They bought extra food and other essential items, such as soap and candles. But war never came. Kennedy convinced Khrushchev to remove the missiles from Cuba, ending the scariest period of the Cold War. Life in Berlin returned to normal—or as normal as it could be with the presence of the Berlin Wall in the heart of the city.

FACTS AND FIGURES OF THE BERLIN WALL	
Total length:	96 miles (154 km)
Maximum height:	12 feet (3.6 m)
Length between East and West Berlin:	26¾ miles (43 km)
Number of watchtowers:	302
Number of guards:	Approximately 14,000
Number of escapees:	Approximately 5,000
Number of persons killed trying to escape:	239
First person killed trying to escape:	Gunter Litwin (August 24, 1961)
Last person killed trying to escape:	Chris Gueffroy (February 6, 1989)

In June 1963, President Kennedy traveled to West Germany. He wanted to assure the people there that the United States would always defend them against the Soviet Union. He also traveled to West Berlin to deliver a similar message. Speaking in front of 250,000 West Berliners on June 26, 1963, Kennedy said:

Freedom has many difficulties, and democracy is not perfect, but we have never had to put a wall up to keep our people in, to prevent them from leaving us. ... When all are free, then we can look forward to that day when this city will be joined as one and this country and this great continent of Europe in a peaceful and hopeful globe. ... All free men, wherever they may live, are citizens of Berlin, and, therefore, as a free man, I take pride in the words Ich bin ein Berliner *["I am a Berliner"].*

During his trip to West Berlin, John F. Kennedy visited Checkpoint Charlie and signed autographs for grateful Germans.

A few months later, Kennedy was shot and killed in Dallas, Texas. Lyndon Johnson became the next U.S. president to carry on the Cold War. ◣

The Shadow of the Wall

Despite the risks, some East Germans were desperate to get past the Berlin Wall and into West Berlin. At times they had help. In 1962, a group of Western college students dug a tunnel that ran from a deserted home in East Berlin to a factory in West Berlin. On September 14, 1962, 26 people used the tunnel to reach the West. *The New York Times* reported on their escape:

> *In their wet and mud-spattered clothing and in their expression of relief, there was a telling indictment of life under communism. That they would take such risks and hardships to escape spoke for itself.*

Another famous tunnel builder was Wolfgang "Tunnel" Fuchs. He built seven tunnels during the early years of the Berlin Wall. His last was finished in the fall of 1964. More than 100 people used it to escape.

The East Germans began destroying more buildings near the Berlin Wall so the diggers would not be able to hide their activities. Only the most loyal Communists were allowed to live in the buildings that remained near the Berlin Wall.

East Berliners escaped through a tunnel that led into West Berlin.

East Germans, with Western help, tried other ways to escape. Some people crammed into cars driven by West Germans or diplomats who had a legal right to travel between the two halves of Berlin. A West German named Horst Breistoffer drove a tiny Italian car back and forth across the border. He assumed the guards would think the car was too small to carry an escapee. Breistoffer, however, had created enough hidden space in the car to transport one person at a time. He made nine successful trips smuggling East Berliners into the West. To try to stop escapes by car, the guards used mirrors to look beneath the vehicles. The mirrors would help the guards spot escapees hidden underneath cars. The guards also ripped up seats and used heat detectors in their searches.

As some East Berliners continued to try to escape, the East German government kept adding to the Berlin Wall. By 1966, it had built several hundred watchtowers along the wall. Separated relatives lost any visual contact they once had with each other.

The wall also passed through rivers and canals. Guards in boats kept watch on these waterways, and rails under the water blocked the path of boats trying to cross to the other side. Later more barbed wire was added, and in 1971 the East Germans put up automatic guns along the border between their country and West Germany. People trying to escape tripped over wires that made the guns fire.

Former Berlin Mayor Willy Brandt became the leader of West Germany in 1969 and tried to improve relations with the East Germans and the Soviets. This effort was called Ostpolitik, or "opening to the East." In 1971, Brandt's work led to a new agreement between the Allies and the Soviet Union. The Soviets agreed for the first time that West Berlin was diplomatically tied to West Germany and was not part of East Germany. The Soviets also said West Berliners could travel into East Germany and East Berlin. The Allies and the Soviets agreed not to use military force in Berlin. And Brandt became the first West German leader to visit East Germany and recognize it as a separate nation.

With the improved relations, West Berliners began to travel to the East in the last half of 1972. West Berliners could also telephone relatives in East Berlin for the first time in years. In East Germany, however, the leaders were not ready to offer their citizens any new freedoms. Erich Honecker, the builder of the Berlin Wall, was running the country. Through the 1970s, he continued to increase the

WILLY BRANDT

As a young man, Willy Brandt opposed Adolf Hitler and his Nazis. Brandt fled Germany before World War II began and returned after the war ended. Entering politics, he was an aide to Berlin Mayor Ernst Reuter during the first Berlin crisis, the blockade and airlift of 1948–1949. Brandt served on the Berlin City Assembly in June 1953, when Soviet tanks ended protests in East Berlin. He was determined that the two Germanys would one day be reunited as a democratic country. Yet during the early 1970s, when he served as the leader of West Germany, Brandt took a different approach. He accepted the existence of East Germany as a separate nation. That move, he hoped, would reduce some of the Cold War tensions in Europe. For his efforts, Brandt was awarded the Nobel Peace Prize.

Over time, West Berliners came to accept the wall as a part of life, though they resented that it cut them off from friends and family on the other side.

division between East Berlin and West Berlin. East Berliners could not leave their city for West Berlin, and in 1975 a new wall went up even farther into East Berlin. The East Germans also strengthened the original wall and replaced concrete blocks with huge slabs of concrete.

For most East Germans, life was better behind their part of the Iron Curtain than in other nations. Industry was stronger in East Germany than in most other Communist nations. But compared to West Germany and West Berlin, the East Germans suffered. And because they received West German television stations, the East German people knew that life was much better in the West. Dan Lucas was a U.S. Army sergeant in West Berlin from 1977 to 1979. He described life in East Berlin:

> *East Berlin was really depressing. ... The people couldn't have been nicer in the stores ... but I felt sorry for them. ... We'd go into the stores—they had a smell about them, real cheap, and very few things in them. ... It was pitiful ... buildings bombed out, never rebuilt. A lot of it was still awful.*

Conditions were somewhat better outside East Berlin. The Wetzel family of Possneck owned a car and a washing machine and had just bought a home. But a trip to the divided East German capital angered them. Petra Wetzel later said she wondered why the East German government kept people imprisoned behind the wall. The Wetzels decided to make a desperate escape. They returned home and recruited friends, the Strelzyks, to build a hot-air balloon that could carry both families into West Germany. They made the balloon out of fabric and built a heater that ran on propane fuel. On September 29, 1979, the two families boarded their homemade craft and drifted over the border into West Germany. The Wetzels and Strelzyks landed safely and began a new life under democracy.

During the 1980s, Cold War tensions again increased. U.S. President Ronald Reagan called the Soviet Union an "evil empire." Reagan wanted to strengthen the U.S. military and work for freedom around the world. He said that his goal was to toss communism onto the "ash heap of history."

Mikhail Gorbachev came to power in the Soviet Union in 1985. He saw that the Soviet Union lacked the money to match U.S. spending on weapons. He knew his people needed such basics as good food and housing. He called for a *perestroika*, or "restructuring," in the Soviet Union. The Communists had to improve the way they ran the economy and the government. Gorbachev also talked about *glasnost*, or "openness." Slowly he would end limits on what information the government gave the people and how much contact they had with the West.

ANOTHER ESCAPE BY AIR

In 1974, an attorney from Munich, West Germany, hired Barry Meeker to rescue his family. Meeker had flown helicopters for the United States during the Vietnam War. Altogether, he made three flights to pick up East Germans, including the attorney's family, who pretended to be on vacation in neighboring Czechoslovakia. On his final mission, in 1975, Meeker had to leave two people behind after Czech soldiers opened fire on his copter. Meeker was slightly wounded, but he managed to escape. On the way back to the West, Meeker had to land before reaching Munich because he was running low on fuel. The helicopter landed just before it ran out of fuel. Meeker survived that close call, but he wasn't as lucky seven years later. In 1982, he was killed when a helicopter he was flying blew up over Oklahoma.

· Over the next two years, Reagan and Gorbachev met several times. They discussed limiting the production of certain nuclear weapons. The two men got along well, and the worst of the Cold War seemed to be behind the United States and the Soviet Union. But Reagan knew the Soviets could do more to promote freedom. On June 12, 1987, Reagan visited West Berlin. He gave a speech that was broadcast all over Europe, including East Berlin. Reagan addressed himself to the Soviet leader:

> *General Secretary Gorbachev, if you seek peace, if you seek prosperity for the Soviet Union and Eastern Europe, if you seek liberalization [the ending of restrictions]: Come here to this gate! Mr. Gorbachev, open this gate! Mr. Gorbachev, tear down this wall!*

By 1989, Communist countries of Eastern Europe were acting on Gorbachev's policies of glasnost and perestroika. Erich Honecker, however, remained a dedicated Communist who opposed such freedoms. The East German people disagreed with Honecker, and soon their actions would lead to drastic changes.

United Again

In late 1989, thousands of people started peaceful protest marches in Leipzig, East Germany. On October 2, about 15,000 people filled the streets there. Erich Honecker considered sending in troops to stop the next week's march, which drew 70,000 people. He wanted the troops to fire on the marchers, but local leaders refused to give the order.

In between the two protests that took place in Leipzig, Soviet President Mikhail Gorbachev came to East Berlin to celebrate the 40th anniversary of the founding of East Germany. Honecker chose several thousand loyal Communists to greet the Soviet leader, but they, too, wanted change.

Gorbachev later recalled what happened on that day:

> *They started chanting slogans: 'Gorby help us!' [Mieczyslaw] Rakowski the Polish leader came up to us and said, 'Do you understand German?' I said, 'I do, a little bit.' 'Can you hear?' I said, 'I can.' He said, 'This is the end.' And that was the end: The regime was doomed.*

East Germany's Communist Party leaders soon replaced Honecker with Egon Krenz. He promised to reform the government, but the East Germans wanted more. On November 4, about 500,000 people marched in East Berlin. They were no longer afraid.

Over the next few days, Krenz proposed a new law to let East Germans travel to other countries. On November 9, 1989, an East German official was asked when the new law would take effect. He replied, "Well, as far as I can see, ... immediately."

In late 1989, East Germans filled the streets of Leipzig to peacefully protest Communist rule.

When that news spread, East Berliners flocked to the guarded checkpoints along the Berlin Wall. The guards did not have orders to let anyone cross into West Berlin. But the crowds kept growing, and finally, at 10:30 P.M., the officer at one of the checkpoints gave the order to throw open the gates. As the East Berliners rushed through, West Berliners greeted them with tears, cheers, and champagne. All the emotions of being separated—and for the East Germans, imprisoned—now turned to joy.

On the first day the wall was open, about 800,000 East Germans crossed over into West Berlin. Happy Berliners from both sides chipped away pieces of the wall with hammers and chisels and swung sledgehammers into the concrete. Many of them kept the pieces as souvenirs. Then, after celebrating their new freedom, most East Berliners

East and West Berliners stormed the Berlin Wall near the Brandenburg Gate on November 9, 1989.

Two Sides to the Wall

When East Berliners were finally allowed to enter West Berlin, they saw a colorful sight. West Berlin artists had painted the wall with brightly colored images and marked it with graffiti. The art appeared after Erich Honecker rebuilt the wall in 1975. The new concrete slabs were large and smooth, giving the artists a perfect canvas for their work. The art and graffiti included a tribute to Soviet President Mikhail Gorbachev, comments on the Cold War, and scenes from everyday life. On their side of the wall, the East Berliners had seen only white concrete. East Germany kept the wall white so it would be easier to spot people approaching it who were hoping to escape.

went home. They did not need to stay in the West, because they believed their freedom would last. And they were right.

In March 1990, East Germany held its first free elections. The people voted the Communist Party out of power. The new government decided to reunite East Germany with West Germany. World maps would now show just one Germany, and soon its capital would once again be an undivided Berlin.

In Berlin, residents rang a replica of the Liberty Bell, a symbol of freedom that had been a gift from the United States. Just a little more than a year later, Gorbachev would end the Communist government in the Soviet Union. By the end of 1991, the Cold War was over. By 1994, U.S., British, and French troops paraded through Berlin for the last time. They finally went home, ending almost 50 years of foreign military presence in Germany's capital.

For East Germans, the change from communism to democracy and capitalism was not easy. The East German economy was much weaker than West Germany's. After reunification, many East German factories shut down, and people lost their jobs. Under communism, the government had always given everyone jobs and kept prices low. Now, out-of-work East Germans struggled to pay for food and other basic items. They also had to adapt to Western goods and attitudes. The West Germans renamed streets and buildings, and in some cases they took control of hospitals and schools. Some East German professionals, such as lawyers, had to relearn their jobs, since the legal system in the West differed so much from the communist system.

The reunification also revealed new information about the past. West German officials opened the files of the Stasi. Many Germans learned that friends and relatives—people they trusted—had been reporting their actions and words to the Stasi. Many of the Stasi spies were sent to prison, as were guards who had shot people trying to escape over the Berlin Wall. Arrests included those of the two men convicted of shooting Peter Fechter in 1962.

The effort to reunite the two Germanys and Berlin has been costly. The German government still spends billions of dollars each year to help the economy in eastern Germany. The city of Berlin alone has a debt of more than $70 billion. The effort to make eastern Germany as modern as the former West Germany has weakened the overall

German economy. Some western Germans are not happy with this effort to rebuild the eastern part of the country, and the Easterners know it.

Despite economic problems, Berlin is now a vibrant city. New buildings have gone up in what was once the Death Strip. East German police and West German soldiers tore down most of the wall. Much of the concrete was crushed and used to pave new roads. Only a few bits of the Berlin Wall remain standing.

On the streets of Berlin, two rows of bricks set in the ground mark where the Berlin Wall once snaked through the city. A small museum stands at what was once Checkpoint Charlie. The museum and the memory of the Berlin Wall are reminders of the world at the time of the Cold War era. For more than 40 years, the world feared the United States and the Soviet Union might wage a devastating world war. In the end, the West's faith in freedom defeated the tyranny of the Iron Curtain. ◣

Timeline

September 1, 1939

Germany invades Poland, beginning World War II.

June 22, 1941

Germany invades the Soviet Union.

May 7, 1945

Germany surrenders, ending World War II in Europe.

May 8, 1945

Berlin is divided into four sectors: the American, British, and French sectors in the West and the Soviet sector in the East.

July 17–August 2, 1945

Allied leaders make their final plans for the division of Germany.

March 5, 1946

British Prime Minister Winston Churchill gives his "Iron Curtain" speech in Fulton, Missouri.

December 19, 1947

U.S. President Harry Truman asks Congress to begin funding the Marshall Plan to aid Europe.

June 24, 1948

The Soviet Union begins a blockade of West Berlin.

June 26, 1948

Allied planes begin the Berlin Airlift.

April 4, 1949

The United States and 11 other countries form the North Atlantic Treaty Organization (NATO).

May 12, 1949

The Soviet Union ends its blockade of West Berlin.

May 23, 1949

The Federal Republic of Germany (West Germany) is created.

August 29, 1949

The Soviet Union tests its first nuclear weapon.

October 7, 1949

The German Democratic Republic (East Germany) is created.

June 25, 1950

North Korea invades South Korea, starting the Korean War.

March 5, 1953

Soviet leader Joseph Stalin dies.

June 17, 1953

Several thousand workers protest in East Berlin.

November 10, 1958

Soviet leader Nikita Khrushchev suggests that Allied troops leave West Berlin.

September 15, 1959

Khrushchev arrives in the United States to meet with President Dwight Eisenhower.

May 1, 1960

The Soviet Union shoots down a U.S. U-2 spy plane.

March 29, 1961

 East German leader Walter Ulbricht first proposes a barrier between East and West Berlin to halt the flow of East Germans into the West.

April 17, 1961

Cuban rebels receiving U.S. aid begin the Bay of Pigs invasion.

June 3–4 1961

U.S. President John F. Kennedy meets with Khrushchev in Vienna, Austria, to discuss growing tensions over Berlin.

August 5, 1961

Khrushchev gives Ulbricht permission to erect a barrier between East and West Berlin.

August 9, 1961

Almost 2,000 people enter the Marienfelde Refugee Center—the most for a single day in 1961.

August 10, 1961

Oleg Penkovsky, a Soviet military officer spying for the Allies, learns about plans to build the Berlin barrier.

August 13, 1961

 East German soldiers and police officers begin erecting a barbed-wire fence between East and West Berlin.

August 14, 1961

Several thousand West Berliners gather to protest the barrier.

August 15, 1961

East Germans begin building a concrete wall between East and West Berlin.

August 16, 1961

About 250,000 people gather to hear West Berlin Mayor Willy Brandt criticize the building of the wall and call on the United States to do something about it.

August 23, 1961

East German officials force West Berliners to get a special pass before they can enter East Berlin.

August 24, 1961

Gunter Litwin is the first East German shot and killed while trying to escape to West Berlin.

Timeline

October 28, 1961

Soviet and U.S. tanks face each other at Checkpoint Charlie but retreat before shots are fired.

August 1962

East Germans begin building a second wall 100 yards (91 m) behind the first one, creating an empty area called the Death Strip.

September 14, 1962

Twenty-six East Berliners escape to the West through a tunnel under the Berlin Wall.

October 22, 1962

President Kennedy informs Americans that the Soviet Union has placed nuclear missiles in Cuba and demands that Khrushchev remove them.

June 26, 1963

Kennedy goes to West Berlin and gives his "Ich bin ein Berliner" speech.

September 3, 1971

The Quadripartite Agreement officially makes East and West Berlin separate countries, and East Berlin is recognized as the capital of East Germany.

September 29, 1979

Two East German families use a homemade hot-air balloon to fly into West Germany.

March 10, 1985

Mikhail Gorbachev becomes the leader of the Soviet Union.

June 12, 1987

U.S. President Ronald Reagan goes to West Berlin and insists that Gorbachev tear down the Berlin Wall.

October 9, 1989

About 70,000 East Germans gather in Leipzig, East Germany, to protest Communist rule in their country.

November 4, 1989

Approximately 500,000 protesters fill the streets of East Berlin.

November 9, 1989

East German officials open the Berlin Wall, allowing their citizens free access to West Berlin.

March 18, 1990

East Germany holds its first free elections; voters force the Communist Party from power.

June 22, 1990

Checkpoint Charlie is removed.

October 3, 1990

East and West Germany unite.

ON THE WEB

For more information on this topic, use FactHound.

1 Go to *www.facthound.com*

2 Type in this book ID: 0756533309

3 Click on the *Fetch It!* button. FactHound will find the best Web sites for you.

HISTORIC SITES

International Spy Museum
800 F St. N.W.
Washington, DC 20004
202/393-7798

This museum's collection includes information on Cold War spies and spy tools used in Berlin and around the world.

The Greenbrier Bunker
300 W. Main St.
White Sulphur Springs, WV 24986
800/453-4858

This underground bunker was built during the Cold War. U.S. leaders would have gone there for safety if a nuclear war had begun.

LOOK FOR MORE BOOKS IN THIS SERIES

Black Tuesday:
Prelude to the Great Depression

A Day Without Immigrants:
Rallying Behind America's Newcomers

Freedom Rides:
Campaign for Equality

The March on Washington:
Uniting Against Racism

The National Grape Boycott:
A Victory for Farmworkers

The Teapot Dome Scandal:
Corruption Rocks 1920s America

Third Parties:
Influential Political Alternatives

89

A complete list of **Snapshots in History** titles is available on our Web site: *www.compasspointbooks.com*

Glossary

allies
friends or helpers; when capitalized, refers to the United States and its allies during major wars

ammunition
material that is fired from a weapon

barricades
things set up to block passage into an area

blockade
military effort to keep goods from entering and leaving a region

capitalism
economic system that allows people to freely create businesses and own as much property as they can afford

corridor
narrow strip of land through a foreign country

democratic
government system run by officials elected by citizens

dictator
ruler who takes complete control of a country, often unjustly

diplomatic
relating to the efforts between countries to keep good relations and end problems

economy
the way a country produces, distributes, and uses its money, goods, natural resources, and services

intelligence
information secretly gathered by spies or electronic devices

nuclear
relating to the core, or nucleus, of tiny bits of matter called atoms; pertaining to or involving atomic weapons

prime minister
in many nations, the head of government

propaganda
information or ideas, some true and some untrue, which are deliberately spread among the public to try to influence their thinking

rationed
given out in limited amounts

refugees
people forced to flee their homelands because of war, persecution, or natural disaster

S-Bahn
the above-ground railway system in Germany

socialism
economic system in which the government owns most businesses

U-Bahn
the German underground railway system

Source Notes

Chapter 1

Page 8, line 11: Curtis Cate. *The Ides of August: The Berlin Wall Crisis, 1961.* New York: M. Evans and Company, 1978, p. 237.

Page 11, line 1: "The Wall." *Cold War.* CNN.com. 2006. 14 Aug. 2006. www.cnn.com/SPECIALS/cold.war/episodes/09/script.html

Page 12, sidebar: Peter Wyden. *Wall: The Inside Story of Divided Berlin.* New York: Simon & Schuster, 1989, p. 161.

Chapter 2

Page 24, sidebar: Jeremy Isaacs and Taylor Downing. *Cold War: An Illustrated History, 1945–1991.* Boston: Little, Brown and Company, 1998, p. 31.

Page 24, line 5: "Iron Curtain." *Cold War.* CNN.com. 2006. 14 Aug. 2006. www.cnn.com/SPECIALS/cold.war/episodes/02/interviews/clifford/

Page 26, line 13: "Race for the Superbomb." *American Experience.* PBS.org. 2004. 14 Aug. 2006. www.pbs.org/wgbh/amex/bomb/peopleevents/pandeAMEX49.html

Chapter 3

Page 30, line 14: Robert P. Grathwol and Donita M. Moorhus. *Berlin and the American Military: A Cold War Chronicle.* New York: New York University Press, 1999, p. 68.

Page 34, line 3: "After Stalin." *Cold War.* CNN.com. 2006. 15 Aug. 2006. www.cnn.com/SPECIALS/cold.war/episodes/07/script.html

Page 35, line 22: Donald P. Steury, ed. *On the Front Lines of the Cold War: Documents on the Intelligence War in Berlin, 1946 to 1961.* Center for the Study of Intelligence, Central Intelligence Agency. 1999. 14 Aug. 2006. www.cia.gov/csi/books/17240/3-4.pdf

Page 37, sidebar: "After Stalin."

Page 37, line 3: Jim Dankiewicz. "The East German Uprising of June 17, 1953, and Its Effects on the USSR and Other Nations of Eastern Europe." University of California Santa Barbara History Department. 15 Aug. 2006. www.history.ucsb.edu/faculty/marcuse/classes/133p/133p99/jim1953.993.htm

Chapter 4

Page 43, line 12: Raymond L. Garthoff. *A Journey Through the Cold War.* Washington, D.C.: The Brookings Institution Press, 2001, p. 126.

Page 45, line 10: Ibid., p. 170.

Page 46, line 12: "The Wall."

Page 48, line 1: *Wall: The Inside Story of Divided Berlin,* p. 55.

SOURCE NOTES

Page 48, line 9: "Radio and Television Report to the American People on the Berlin Crisis." 25 July 1961. John F. Kennedy Presidential Library and Museum. 16 Aug. 2006. www.jfklibrary.org/Historical+Resources/Archives/Reference+Desk/Speeches/JFK/003POF03BerlinCrisis07251961.htm

Page 49, line 21: *Wall: The Inside Story of Divided Berlin,* pp. 81–82.

Chapter 5
Page 52, line 17: Ibid., p. 93.

Page 52, sidebar: Ibid., p. 23.

Page 55, line 3: "USA and USSR: Exchange of Notes on the Berlin Wall, 1961." Modern History Sourcebook. 2001. 16 Aug. 2006. www.fordham.edu/halsall/mod/1961berlin-usa-ussr.html

Page 58, line 6: "Interview with Margit Hosseini" 17 Aug. 2006. www.gwu.edu/~nsarchiv/coldwar/interviews/episode-9/hosseni2.html

Page 58, line 22: "The Wall."

Chapter 6
Page 65, line 3: Ibid.

Page 67, line 1: *Cold War: An Illustrated History*, p. 183.

Page 69, line 21: *Wall: The Inside Story of Divided Berlin*, p. 277.

Page 71, line 1: "Text: Kennedy's Berlin Speech." BBC News. 26 June 2003. 18 Aug. 2006. http://news.bbc.co.uk/1/hi/world/europe/3022166.stm

Chapter 7
Page 72, line 9: William F. Buckley. *The Fall of the Berlin Wall.* New York: John Wiley and Sons, 2004, p. 88.

Page 77, line 8: *Berlin and the American Military: A Cold War Chronicle*, p. 145.

Page 78, lines 5 and 11: *Cold War: An Illustrated History*, p. 334.

Page 79, line 11: "Remarks at the Brandenburg Gate West Berlin, Germany June 12, 1987." Ronald Reagan Presidential Foundation and Library. 19 Aug. 2006. www.reaganfoundation.org/reagan/speeches/speech.asp?spid=25

Chapter 8
Page 81, line 1: "The Wall Comes Down." *Cold War.* CNN.com. 2006. 19 Aug. 2006. www.cnn.com/SPECIALS/cold.war/episodes/23/script.html

Page 81, line 17: "The Fall of the Berlin Wall," Berlin Wall Online. 20 Aug. 2006. www.dailysoft.com/berlinwall/history/fall-of-berlinwall.htm

SELECT BIBLIOGRAPHY

Brandt, Willy. *My Life in Politics.* London: Hamish Hamilton, 1992.

Buckley, William F., Jr. *The Fall of the Berlin Wall.* New York: John Wiley & Sons, 2004.

Cate, Curtis. *The Ides of August: The Berlin Wall Crisis, 1961.* New York: M. Evans and Company, 1978.

Isaacs, Jeremy, and Taylor Downing. *Cold War: An Illustrated History, 1945–1991.* Boston: Little, Brown and Company, 1998.

McCullough, David. *Truman.* New York: Simon & Schuster, 1992.

Paterson, Thomas G., J. Garry Clifford, and Kenneth J. Hagan. *American Foreign Relations: A History Since 1895.* 5th ed. Boston: Houghton Mifflin, 2000.

Schmemann, Serge. *When the Wall Came Down: The Berlin Wall and the Fall of Soviet Communism.* Boston: Kingfisher, 2006.

Wyden, Peter. *Wall: The Inside Story of Divided Berlin.* New York: Simon & Schuster, 1989.

FURTHER READING

Bjornlund, Britta. *The Cold War.* San Diego: Lucent Books, 2002.

Grant, R. G. *The Berlin Wall.* Austin, Texas: Raintree Steck-Vaughn, 1999.

Levy, Patricia. *The Fall of the Berlin Wall, November 9, 1989.* Austin, Texas: Raintree Steck-Vaughn, 2003.

Tracy, Kathleen. *The Fall Of The Berlin Wall.* Hockessin, Del.: Mitchell Lane Publishers, 2005.

Index